First World War
and Army of Occupation
War Diary
France, Belgium and Germany

61 DIVISION
182 Infantry Brigade,
Brigade Trench Mortar Battery
13 June 1916 - 31 August 1916

WO95/3057/4

The Naval & Military Press Ltd
www.nmarchive.com
Published in association with The National Archives

Published by

The Naval & Military Press Ltd

Unit 10 Ridgewood Industrial Park,

Uckfield, East Sussex,

TN22 5QE England

Tel: +44 (0) 1825 749494

www.naval-military-press.com

www.nmarchive.com

This diary has been reprinted in facsimile from the original. Any imperfections are inevitably reproduced and the quality may fall short of modern type and cartographic standards.

© **Crown Copyright**
Images reproduced by permission of The National Archives, London, England, 2015.

Contents

Document type	Place/Title	Date From	Date To
Heading	WO95/3057/4 Brigade Trench Mortar Battery		
Heading	61st Division 182nd Infy Bde Trench Mortar Battery Jun-Aug 1916		
Heading	War Diary Of 182nd Trench Mortar Battery For June 13-30th		
War Diary	Lagorgue	13/06/1916	20/06/1916
War Diary	Laventie	21/06/1916	25/07/1916
War Diary	La Gorque	26/07/1916	30/07/1916
War Diary	Laventie	31/07/1916	31/07/1916
Heading	War Diary Of 182nd Trench Mortar Battery August 1916		
War Diary	Laventie	01/08/1916	31/08/1916

WO 95/BOS 7/4

Brigade Trench Mortar Battery

61ST DIVISION
182ND INFY BDE

TRENCH MORTAR BATTERY
JUN - AUG 1916.

61ST DIVISION
182ND INFY BDE

Vol XI

WAR DIARY
of
182nd TRENCH MORTAR BATTERY

for June 13-30th

June-Aug 16

CONFIDENTIAL

Army Form C. 2118.

WAR DIARY
or
INTELLIGENCE SUMMARY.
(Erase heading not required.)

of the 182nd Trench Mortar Battery

June 1916

Place	Date	Hour	Summary of Events and Information	Remarks and references to Appendices
LA GORGUE	13		182 T.M.B. formed. The following officers are appointed. Lieut G.W.S. Hopkins 2/5 RWarwR to command. Hon J.G. Kay 2/5 RWarwR " R.A. Philippo 2/7 RWarwR 2/Lt W.H. Lynes 2/7 RWarwR The personnel to drawn from 2/5 and 2/7 RWarwR Battery Spent is organising battery and drawing our stores etc	
	14		" "	
	15		" "	
	16		On 3" STOKES MORTAR teams are from 183rd Inf Bnig. arrived LAVENTIE for instructional purposes.	
	17		} Spent in drills and instruction. On the 18th was to receive 7 more	
	18		} Stokes Mortars, thus completing our establishment (8 guns)	
	19		} Lieut G.W.S. Hopkins promoted Capt.	
	20			

Army Form C. 2118.

WAR DIARY
or
INTELLIGENCE SUMMARY. 1/182nd Trench Mortar Battery

(Erase heading not required.)

Place	Date	Hour	Summary of Events and Information	Remarks and references to Appendices
LAVENTIE	21		182nd Inf. Bgd. relieved 183rd Inf. Brig. in HUATED GRANGE and NEUVE CHAPELLE Sectors. The 182 T.M.B. relieved the 105th T.M.B. in the front, the latter Battery leaving some few NCO's in the line until the Battery should have settled down. Eight guns were mounted in the line in the following positions:- (1) M30 a 1¾·4 (2) M29 b 8·2 } Left Section (3) M29 d 2·8½ (4) M30 c 1·3 (5) M30 c 1·1 (6) h 35 b 7·1 } Right Section (7) S·5·G 2·9½ (8) S·5 a½ b 0½·7 The Battalions in the line were as follows:- (1) Left 2/7 Rl. Bn. Wk (2) Centre 2/5 Rl. Wk (3) Right 2/8 Rl. Wk The Brigade front extends from ERITH STREET on N. to OXFORD STREET on S. in the line via Le Philippe Left Sector, Lt Keay Right Sector.	

Army Form C. 2118.

WAR DIARY
or
INTELLIGENCE SUMMARY.
(Erase heading not required.)

of A/182nd Trench Mortar Battery.   June 1916

Instructions regarding War Diaries and Intelligence Summaries are contained in F.S. Regs., Part II. and the Staff Manual respectively. Title pages will be prepared in manuscript.

Place	Date	Hour	Summary of Events and Information	Remarks and references to Appendices
LAVENTIE	22		Half the Battery is in the line at a time for 4 days tour. Other remainder in billets at LAVENTIE in Rue du Paradis. Have the line are relieved by C/Battery and took over tour.	
	23		Spent in registering targets and arranging ammunition supply and clearing of line.	
	24			
	25		No firing.	
	26		Enfilade the day at enemy's front line. Combined Artillery and T.M. bombardment of enemy's line. Started at 11.5 pm. a/c (contact.) with 3 guns B section from M.29.d.2.0½ M.30.a.3.1.6. M.30.a.3.0½. in 5 min. Mins bursts. About 170 stells were fired. No (a) no casualties. No details. Gas fully north (station) of line. 12 3.7" T.M. attached to smoke showing a Brigade fear. 2000 smoke bombs taken into the line.	
	28		Intermittent bombardment of enemy's from ours a while brigade from.	
	29		Discharge of smoke by hand and from 3.7" T.M's. at might.	
	30		A quiet day. Bombardment of enemy's front and communication trench.	

P Hopkins Capt.
O/C R/T.M.B.

July 1916

Vol II

WAR DIARY or **INTELLIGENCE SUMMARY** of 182nd Trench Mortar Battery.

Army Form C. 2118.

Place	Date	Hour	Summary of Events and Information	Remarks and references to Appendices
LAVENTIE	1		Night of 30/1 Heavy enemy bombardment in Centre Subsection. During the night Lt. J.G. KEAY was killed by shrapnel. The gun at M.29.c.6.2½ was struck by shrapnel and slight damage was sustained by the elevating stand. The elevating stands belonging to the guns at M.30.c.1.1½ and M.30.c.1.2¼ were removed during the bombardment and hidden in bay opposite by Lt. KEAY. The gun at M.30.c.1.1½ and M.30.c.1.2¼ bombarded enemy craters at BIRDCAGE Sector in the night.	
	2		The enjured gun was removed from M.29.6.2¼ for repairs. During the day all guns at M.24.c.8½.1, M.30.a.1½.4, M.36.a.0.9½, M.35.d.6.9½, S.5.6.15 reported in working order with satisfactory results.	
		11.p.m	Smoke bombs were thrown from 3 3"-7" guns in LEFT Subsection.	
	3		Left group T.M.B. was relieved.	
		4.a.m	T.M.B. personnel were rationed by Battalion in the line. Tea, from this day onwards individual cooking ceased and The elevating stands buried during night 30/1 July. 31/July were found the Battery enclosed for tea. All light mortars in the line repaired or issued for use during the day.	

Army Form C. 2118.

July 1916.

WAR DIARY or INTELLIGENCE SUMMARY.

(Erase heading not required.)

182nd TRENCH MORTAR BATTERY

Place	Date	Hour	Summary of Events and Information	Remarks and references to Appendices
AVENUE	3		At evening stand to guns at M36.a.0.9½ and M35.d.6.9½ fired 15 shells at enemy front line with good results. Shells were observed near at sap line at M36.a.9.3½ mostly on air bursts no front line is occupied at S36.7.9 and were all short. No long distance shelling being available ambush M35.c.5.2 could not be reached.	
	4		Cart were observed to bring well at trench. Total amount of shells fired 24.	
	4	2.45pm	2/8 Rounds selected. Wishbone on north sub group.	
			In the afternoon 12 shells were fired on trench junction near S.T.S.R. and S5.C.2.9 was fair near high load.	
	5		Right group TMB relieved.	
		4 pm	Reported on guns in enemy wire at NCA.	
	6		Gun turned during night fired 30 (28) returned to Camp after being relieved by R.G.A. W3/W3/72.	
		10.15pm	Heavy fire from ltg gun at M30.d... at gun at NCS.	
	7		New Lewis range cartridge arrived to test fire. Reported fair condition on new test firing.	
			M.G. at M36.c.27	
			Left guns T.M.B. relieved	

WAR DIARY or INTELLIGENCE SUMMARY

Army Form C. 2118.

Of 182nd TRENCH MORTAR BATTERY

July 1916

Place	Date	Hour	Summary of Events and Information	Remarks and references to Appendices
AVENUE	8		Registering fire on M.36.a.1.5.6.7. Results satisfactory. Fired number[?] rounds = 17.	
	9	11.9 pm	Right group T.M.B. retired.	
			T.M. Bombardment of enemy lines by 2/5 Division. From 179 L.T.M. registering about 40 rounds at M35.c.2.7.	
			M.36.c.1.1, M.36.c.1.2.3, M.36.d.3 & on M.29.q.1. From 11.13/4 to 12.25. Bursts usually up of ground.	
			M.36.c.1.3 & M.11.30 & 11.24. In all cases the enemy retaliated at 12 trench mortar support in our sap	
			Front only & for what he terminated enemy curtain found. Only two of our reply in 2.1 hr	
			38 gunner M.35 & I were unusually mild - placed just to our rear in the Shell hole 250	
	10.	11.23 pm	Our trench flare mort just N.9.18 BIRDCAGE	
			Guns in back of M.36.a/oc	
			2/5 Division relieved Division in line.	
			124 M.R. M. bombers settled into shifts at M.36.b.8.4, M.9.2 (just 5 from Oxford Road	
			junction of OXFORD STREET.	
			Gunner find on shell dump at Duck's BILL and proceed to occupy it	
			Duck's 13. Report for a gun.	
			Left gun T.M.B. relieved	
	11		Guns registered on enemy's trench at M.36.a.O.9. with satisfactory results	

July 1916

Army Form C. 2118.

WAR DIARY
or
INTELLIGENCE SUMMARY
of 102nd TRENCH MORTAR BATTERY

(Erase heading not required.)

Instructions regarding War Diaries and Intelligence Summaries are contained in F.S. Regs., Part II. and the Staff Manual respectively. Title pages will be prepared in manuscript.

Place	Date	Hour	Summary of Events and Information	Remarks and references to Appendices
LAVENTIE	11	5 pm	Also as to the new crater blown by the enemy at Duck's Bill. The gun at M.35 to open fire. Very rapidly got its range after which it was subjected to bursts of rapid fire. The shells were observed to burst well within the crater.	
			The extreme Right Gun aft Battery reported enemy's trench at S.56.74. Result Accurate open trench.	
	12		Fired at enemy's front line at S.5.6,9.6. Also at an M.G. at S.6.7.8½ which was located by th. infantry. Results in both cases were good, things in to look pretty obviously. Crater to accordance.	
		10pm	Fired a burst of 3 rounds rapid followed by 3 rounds at 5 minutes intervals into enemy's new crater at Duck's Bill. The following seen to burst well inside crater. Enemy fire line at M.30 S.5. and M.30.C.5.5. were also brought under fire.	
			Today 3 gun 3.7" guns were sent to LA GORGUE to repair.	
	4	4 pm	A meeting of intelligence officers at Bulford. It was pointed out that Stokes gun External initial difficulties experienced by the Commanding officer causing gun faults. It was also the importance of an infantry company commanders account of given accurate information and knowing of supply, ing to the Stokes gun.	

WAR DIARY or INTELLIGENCE SUMMARY

Army Form C. 2118.

of 182nd TRENCH MORTAR BATTERY

Place	Date	Hour	Summary of Events and Information	Remarks and references to Appendices
LAVENTIE	13		Total number of shells fired 30. We harassed the enemy's front line from M.30.a.5.1. to M.30.a.5.2. and also from M.30.c.9.4. to M.30.a.5.3. It was thought that the snipers but and if not men afta grenade battoons in the area. The effect of the shooting was to burst on shelter and parapet; [illegible] rounds were half brown accurate, all firing taking place at night.	
		11.30 pm	Acting in accordance with a Time-table drawn up by C/O 4/8 Royals we fired a burst of rapid rate at enemy's new crater at Duck's Bill when he was reported to have a working-party out. The burst was repeated at 12.30 and again at 1.45 am. It was thought that the party was dispersed. The Stella was [illegible] very true which the enemy could fire was [illegible] slightly. There was moderate retaliation with "whizz bangs."	
	14		Total shells fired 10 at (1) Support rifle grenade battery at M.30.a.1.4.	
			(2) " Sniper's nest at M.30.b.2.3. Result: Direct observ. hit on point aimed at.	
			(3) Working party at M.30.c.5.7. The party was dispersed.	

WAR DIARY
or
INTELLIGENCE SUMMARY. of 182nd Trench Mortar Battery

Army Form C. 2118.

July 1916

(Erase heading not required.)

Instructions regarding War Diaries and Intelligence Summaries are contained in F.S. Regs., Part II. and the Staff Manual respectively. Title pages will be prepared in manuscript.

Place	Date	Hour	Summary of Events and Information	Remarks and references to Appendices
LAVENTIE	15		Orders were received to move the Left 1/2 Battery into the FAUQUISSART Sector old emplacements being taken over by 92nd T.M.B. These were carried over and to a point before with 250 rounds were moved into the new position before evening. The new emplacements were as follows N.13.c.1.2, N.13.c.4.9, N.13.c.5.5. N.13.c.8.7½. The Right 1/2 Battery was ordered to hand over to the 94" T.M.B. at some date not clear upon, but the 94"T.M.B. not arriving a 1st of Left Battery seen to in our old position. During night 15/16 89 trench mortars in FAUQUISSART sector fired 121 rounds on the enemy's parapet during the destroyal of Gas fear on our front line.	
	16		With a view to offensive operation at FAUQUISSART from the Right 1/2 Battery moved their guns to new positions as follows M.24.D.4.9.½, M.24.b.5.½, M.24.b.7.½ and N.13.c.8.2. Our new emplacements were M.24.b.5.1 was built during the day. Left half battery also had many shells were made while it is hoped over 300 shells were brought up into line giving a total store of some 700 shells. No attack took place owing to preparation of our during the night 15/17.	
	17		Operations from front Panel at offers of 1st Rifle Brigade was owner of trench. Lt Col Left half battery came relieved. Saw by machine gun covering at wire ledge. Battery of 4 guns 1 officer and 10 O.R.	

WAR DIARY
or
INTELLIGENCE SUMMARY of 182nd Trench Mortar Battery

July 1916

Army Form C. 2118.

Place	Date	Hour	Summary of Events and Information	Remarks and references to Appendices
LAVENTIE	18		The guns at N.13.c.12, N.13.c.4¼, N.13.c.4¾, N.13.c.55, N.13.c.8.7½ registered during the day, but orders were issued to save ammunition. (As the enemy instruction was pour le 4 juin on the right half Battery the mortars were partially used, & the mortar in the position at morning 17 & 19th. A trench mortar by 100 shells was called up to ERITH [railhead] in the evening.	
	19		The Battery Commanders in the attack made upon the German line by the 2/6 and 2/7 R.Warwick. Fire zero fire until just before the assault & mortars kept up a steady accurate fire upon the enemy's front line and support. Early in the afternoon the emplacement at M.24.d.5.9½ was blown in by shell fire, so too only 7 guns could be used during the assault of the bombardment. Just previous to the assault all 7 gun pits two mortars cracked their firmly supporting the range by it was very long between cartridges posts to steady infantry [slowly] to advance. By the time every shell in the [ ] was expended A battery [ ] fired rather over 700 rounds. It halted [ ] to find a gun tripod with the 2/6 R.Warwick, if possible, but their tripod & rest of brittle [ ] attempt being made. Even (as they succeeded) it is returned doubtful what a general have been able to accomplish owing to the exhaustion of ammunition after complete absence of all available trench mortars in supply ammunition. At about 10 p.m. 1 gun	

Army Form C. 2118.

WAR DIARY
or
INTELLIGENCE SUMMARY.
(Erase heading not required.)

Place	Date	Hour	Summary of Events and Information	Remarks and references to Appendices
	20		ordered guns to be repaired & officers & officers staff. (The guns are found sinister expressly fire but complete guns exit - months of battery table & various tempered shields. The guns were fairly left out to the personnel at GRANT'S POST. All attempt to approach the battery delayed not gives the any gun to open the release capacity despite very accurate shoots and fire of Enemy Guns (one luckily was very high, a superior expanded by enemy). The emplacements were blown in but the guns were retrieved. Subsequent efforts and chance to batter guns approach to the emplacement [illegible] [illegible] & [illegible] not selfs assured). Under orders reconn[aissance] Brigade I withdrew about one & half a [illegible] & officer and 70 men who were left out of guns at GRANT'S POST, but every [illegible] [illegible] four of 300 shells to be rail[ed] bundles, these to install [illegible] at the site of the present enemy.	
	21.		The day was spent in distributing ammunits to emplacement. Later evening orders were received to remove the guns and turn from GRANT'S POST. This was done at her sleeping forts [illegible] at L'Esprits Fort Sta.	

Army Form C. 2118.

WAR DIARY
or
INTELLIGENCE SUMMARY.

of 182nd Trench Mortar Battery

July 1916

(Erase heading not required.)

Place	Date	Hour	Summary of Events and Information	Remarks and references to Appendices
LAVENTIE	22		Early in day four guns together with 1 officer and their teams were instructed to be ready to reinforce the Battery going into the Line at LAVENTIE. Some firing was done with enemy's parapet at WICK SALIENT at N13 d 2.5, and N13 c 9.2 and also at N13 c 8½.1 with satisfactory results. 12 shells expended.	
	23		Orders received. Move with reserves to LA GORGUE. A/Trs 4 guns (half with 1 officer and 24 men in billets proceeded to LA GORGUE at midday and occupied the old billets. The remaining 4 guns already relief unit two. By evening the whole 4 guns in the line relieved. 183 T.M.B. Battery was in billets at LA GORGUE.	
	24			
	25	3pm	Inspection of Battery by G.O.C. Division, Maj. Gen. COLIN MACKENZIE in the field opposite Bde H.Q. The men turned up in frames, steel guns, aligned in turn. A call in turn full march use was made of the carriers. The Battery were complimented by the G.O.C. Divn upon its work in the Trenches.	

Army Form C. 2118.

WAR DIARY
or
INTELLIGENCE SUMMARY.

July 1916   1/182nd Trench Mortar Battery

(Erase heading not required.)

Place	Date	Hour	Summary of Events and Information	Remarks and references to Appendices
LA GORGUE	26		Ordinary routine training continues. Gun drill, physical drill, some shoemaker and armourer duty, with a gymnastic week before breakfast. Guns and carts were thoroughly cleaned, and in the afternoon the men were bathed at Div^l baths	
	27		Routine work as above	
	28		Routine as above. To-day 5 men of 2/8 R.Works joined the Battery. We are still 6 under establishment but no further accounts can be spared at present.	
	29		Inspected at work by Major Poole of Divisional Staff. He made several valuable suggestions for training, especially with regard to digging the guns under cover, and also desired to see methods of carrying loads. Much remains to be settled in this respect.	
	30		Sunday. In the morning Church Parade. In the afternoon Brigade Horse Show was held. We entered a team for the Tug of War and drew the favourite the 2/5 R.Works. Owing to the non-appearance of one horse we had to scratch.	

Army Form C. 2118.

July 1916

WAR DIARY
or
INTELLIGENCE SUMMARY.
(Erase heading not required.)

of 182nd Trench Mortar Battery

Place	Date	Hour	Summary of Events and Information	Remarks and references to Appendices
LAVENTIE	31		Ordered to relieve 184th T.M.B. in MOATED GRANGE sector on Aug 1. I went to LAVENTIE to take over, whilst other men spent the day cleaning guns, packing stores etc. In the afternoon they went to "D" batts	
		4.30pm	Conference of CO's at Brigade. Defence scheme explained and discussed. New notes for retaining my men over 182 M.G.C. adopted (a new clean on our return but soon blown over to "A" Batt. Q.M. concerned via M.G. limber, is kept labelled with R.E.'Y men and mops requisite. New rates all even sent up with "A" Batt. rations and cooked by Reserve Platoon is bad. Great improvement in gun metal.	

Vol X 3

WAR DIARY
of
182ⁿᵈ Trench Mortar Battery.

August. 1916.

CONFIDENTIAL.

Army Form C. 2118.

WAR DIARY or **INTELLIGENCE SUMMARY.**

of 182nd Trench Mortar Battery

August

Place	Date	Hour	Summary of Events and Information	Remarks and references to Appendices
LAVENTIE	1		To-day we moved the gun LA GORGUE to the line relieving 184 T.M.B. According to the proposed defence scheme at Laventie the 4 guns in the district between the two railway lines at the sector from BIRTH to junction of M.29.3, M.29.2 and him in front, gun position M.29.3, M.29.2 & SIGN POST LANE (a disused house, 1st floor position). One other emplacement is at the Right Sector, one has been destroyed, one partly spoilt, and one will be constructed in the rear. Sector is at Maxwell, 1 6 mm moustache, 2 G 4 guns all cemented 2 T.M. present is the Left Sector is at Taller's Emplacements, M.29.d 7.1, M.24.d 5½ 1½, M.30 a 12.4, M.29 & 2.27. Howitzer in the building. Two emplacements at the Rifle Sector.	
			Reported that all the guns with satisfactory results. 10 shots being fired.	
	2		To-day we fired 20 shells at enemy's activies. Lavency at Trench and mask, front parapet.	
	3		We fired at enemy's listening post between M.30 a 3½ and M.32 a 4.0, at houses between M.30 a 1½ and M.30 a 5.5, a bay of front sea of his sapping state are ?just ?? open to enemy trench at M.30 a 5.7 and at his sapheads at M.29 & 55. We fired at the lookout opposite at M.30 a 5.7 and at his sapheads at M.29 & 55. The enemy did not reply.	
			Received notification at M 7am & again ½ clip ?? troop.	
			The men behaved ?well and ? in ? of latter is of two who are very satisfactory.	

Army Form C. 2118.

WAR DIARY
or
INTELLIGENCE SUMMARY. of 182nd Trench Mortar Battery

(Erase heading not required.)

Place	Date	Hour	Summary of Events and Information	Remarks and references to Appendices
LAVENTIE	4		We fired 15 shells (1) Traversing school trench for line from M30 a 5.3½ to M30 a 6½.5.	
			(2) At man edge of crater at M30 a 5½.7	
			(3) Communication trench at M24d 7.1½	
			(4) " M30 a 0½.1½	
			Results were good all shells bursting well in the target with the exception of "Duds" was extremely low.	
	5	7.30pm	T.M's collaborate with M.T.M's and 18 pdrs from a screen's front line from M30 a 5.5 to M30 a 5.7. and on his support line from M30 a 5.3 0½ to M30 c 5.9½. They continued with deliberate fire during the whole period of M.T.M. activity. The enemy retaliated with medium and light T.M. opposite M29.4. B.2.2.	
			Total number of shells fired 36.	
	6		We fired 16 shots suitably enemy's front line from M30 a 3½.4 to M30 a 5.3. Also firing on front line at M29.d 4½. 0½. The enemy retaliated a rifle at M30 a 1½.4 and whiz bangs also of which fell short, and from trench mo near M24.d 1.5, left 3 rounds, of shrapnel during no arrangement.	
			In the evening as ordered to travelly onward the enemy's trench clearly the ground for reports to sappers	
			Gauge of base cap screw having become stripped.	

WAR DIARY
or
INTELLIGENCE SUMMARY.

1/82nd Trench Mortar Batty.

Army Form C. 2118.

Place	Date	Hour	Summary of Events and Information	Remarks and references to Appendices
LAVENTIE	7		Shots fired 6/0. 8G/5.15. (1) Front and Sapphir line at M.30.d.4.1. with good effect. We provoked retaliation with rifle grenades and H.E. which considerably damaged our firebays about M.29.b.7½.4. (2) We continued worrying enemy front line between M.30.d.4.9 and M.30.a.5.5. from 11 a.m. to 4 p.m. provoking retaliation in shape of 3 rifle grenades which fell behind our firebays on our H.E. into our wire. (3) Sapphir's Sap at M.29.d. 6½. 3½. Result, retaliation with 6 rifle grenades about 15 yds behind our line and above (5 seconds). Shots fired also behind our line. Total of all guns we carried out a systematic interval and continued fire at our military posts.	
	8		Today our new emplacement at M.35.d.6.9. (Bay 9) was completed. Last night the enemy blew a big crater at M.30.c.2.5. as a result of which we were requested by Battalion Commander to keep it his guards. We fired 10 shots reporting a new target at M.30.a.4.5. purely retaliation into L.T.M. and H.E. on WINCHESTER TRENCH. We also fired at intervals between 4.30 and 7pm on Saphead at M.24.d.6½.3.	
	9		Today 104 T.M.B. took over our emplacement N. of WINCHESTER TRENCH. An accident with the cart. Battalion Orders and to entrain into NEUVE CHAPELLE Sect.	

WAR DIARY or INTELLIGENCE SUMMARY

Army Form C. 2118.

of 182nd Trench Mortar Battery

Place	Date	Hour	Summary of Events and Information	Remarks and references to Appendices
LAVENTIE	10		Again at request of O.C. 2/7 R.Warw. we carried on trip to B.Shots in trees of the numerous enemy posts opposite our line at M30.a.9. resulting in good bursts in the trees. Today we moved two guns into the NEUVE CHAPELLE Sector to emplacements at M33d 6½.9½ & S.5.6.2.9. and S.5.6.0½.6½. & a third gun was taken up to run LAVENTIE to an emplacement, but owing to several enemy fortnightly? winds it was removed to an emplacement at M33d 6½.9½. Our newlaid S.Guns in the end.	
	11		Our H LEFT we fired 15 Sh.o.6 on front line at M30 & S.5.½. Arrangement has been made to fire during the night 10/11 as a suprise work, fuses on C/G M30 a.S.5. but the programme was carried by O/C 2/6 R.War.R. & we fired 122 shells desperately not M.T.M.s and 10 Stokes from 5-5.30 pm, the return fire coming heavy? being Maps? S of the area supplied by GOC. Our Stokes bought to rear between M30 c.S.6½ and M30 a.5.2 and N. natures? the line of Communication trench at M35B 3½.4. In N. Mutton sects. we caused an explosion also of a later MINENWERFER whose strumpen? caused fires. on N.Of S. sects we provided interval retaliation with rifle grenades especially in early morning when. by tot bursts of fives S.5.6 and M35.7.9.	

T./134. Wt. W708-776. 500000. 4/15. Sir J. C. & S.

WAR DIARY or INTELLIGENCE SUMMARY

Army Form C. 2118.

9/182nd Trench Mortar Battery
August 1916

Place	Date	Hour	Summary of Events and Information	Remarks and references to Appendices
LAVENTIE	12		Shells fired 140. On 2 N. Craters H30 a 42 to H30 a 5.8. were searched thoroughly to a depth of 50-150 yards for possible retreats of S.M.T.M. trench further direct H30 a 9½ and some rifle grenades. On 3. as fired on ① Communication trench at H35 a 3½ 4½ to a depth of 50 yards. ② Trenches between H35 d 8.2½ and S.5 b 2.9½ and approach for telephone at day in retaliation to enemy H.T.M fire. To enemy T.M fire in the Sally Port positions heavy own Stokes guns are usually in position all night in order to retaliate when required. At night we fired up 201 Stella lts to clear via entrance of WINCHESTER and EUSTON. During the firing on a N trench a a 4326 Pte. BAYLISS H. was slightly wounded in the arm. Shots fired 111. ① On 7.30 pm we cooperated with H.T.M's and 10 pdr. manly fired a barrage from H30 a 4½ to H30 a 5.9. and N. flanks of to bombardt area "Winter" also at M.36 a 3.1½ ② During the day we retaliated to every H.T.M fire & an found. Bombed from H35 d 8.3.2 to S.16 B.O.'s Trench T.T.M fire direct on Tanenbaum. M.S. 5. 6. During the preparation for an H.S. test examined trench with 2 Result three (or ?) to replace to trench locations, all but the largest crater T2 stations is probably not central.	
	13			

WAR DIARY or INTELLIGENCE SUMMARY

of 1/(2nd) Trench Mortar Battery

Army Form C. 2118.

Place	Date	Hour	Summary of Events and Information	Remarks and references to Appendices
LAVENTIE	14		Shots fired 125. (1) Our N sector co-operated with H.T.M's at 8.15 pm on whole line or shifted our fire to it open as reach area from M.30.C.5.d. to M.30.C.5.5. (2) Our S. Sector co-operated with our detachments from available trees mount duty the day installation trained T.M's at top of old abattis envelopes. Opposite sector S.5.5 enemy shellings large quantity of aerial torpedos in our retaliation amounts to five. To-day we sent 1 pm MK II up to D.A.D.O.S. as pattern to be workshops. New mounting on firing mound Little Freddy battery reported.	
	15		Shots fired 101 (1) Our N cor cooperated from 6-6.30 pm with 18 pdrs and M.T.M's firing a barrage of area M.30.c.5.7½ to M.30.c.4⅔a. Results were difficult to observe owing to rain between M.30.c.14.7 and M.30.a.5.5. Our enemy retaliated with 15 aerial torpedoes opposite PURCHASE street & Ripley MINES, and 5 rattes near to ours. (2) During day our Stokes enemy's firing lane at daring opposite sector S.5.6 and M.35. during some retaliation occurred opposite fall in left of S.5.6 awhile of M.35. Opposite Duck's Bill our shells from line at intervals. All my fire was battle up 255 Stella 6 rail as before.	

WAR DIARY or INTELLIGENCE SUMMARY

Army Form C. 2118.

August 1916 of 102nd Trench Mortar Battery

Place	Date	Hour	Summary of Events and Information	Remarks and references to Appendices
LAVENTIE	16		Shots fired 112. (1) On N we cooperated with M.T.M's at 7 p.m and concentrated on a suspected #T.M. about M30.5.1½. Provided retaliation with H.T.M. at sect. M29.3. (2) On S. Cooperated with M.T.M's at 7 p.m firing on commencement line Tgs at M36.a.3.1½. and on front and support lines from M36.a.3.1½ to S.5.6.7.9. drawing retaliation by L2 reverse torpedoes tally at S.5.6.	
	17		Shots fired 139. (1) On N. the enemy have been on 4 H.T.M. at sect. M29.3 in reply to our artillery fire at 6 p.m. We concentrated on fire in M30.c.6½.2½. Been was very retaliation. (2) On S. during day and evening we fired on front and support lines for G.H.E. on about 12 aerial torpedo shells, blew down two or three S.S.S.. We also repaired sufficient enemy M.G. at out MgB, E.21.8. Spelly Wgem, ctl it was firing at our aeroplane. Snam retaliation with 4 few shrapnel and aerial Corpedoes tally shots at sect M.33.3. (a odder, and expended good [wires] 10 iKrel] on H. 35.0 2-9.7) No retaliation. At night details up 135 rounds here Festa.	

WAR DIARY or INTELLIGENCE SUMMARY

Army Form C. 2118.

1/1(2") Trench Mortar Battery

August 1916

LAVENTIE

Date	Hour	Summary of Events and Information	Remarks and references to Appendices
18		2/7 Reworks relieve 2/6 Reworks in LEFT subsector. Shots fired 175. (1) On left M. cooperated with M.T.M's and 8" phm. fires 6-6.30 pm on a fair for 10-16.30 pm firing on enemy front line from M36.a.5.1 to M30.a.6.2, during S./M retaliated with M.T.M. at Sects M.29.3	
		(2) On S. during day we retaliated for aerial torpedoes on Sects 3.5.8. M.G firing from about M35.c.2.1.9	
		In the afternoon we cooperated with arty operation. R/F Reworks fired 3-3.30pm on silent tps.	
	11.5 pm	When 2/8 Reworks raided enemy crater at "Duck's Bill" we fired 8 salvos together from 3 guns associated up at shelling at "Barrier Torpedoes" tkg about 2 suspected emplacements up at M36.a.SL.03 - also one at M38.c.1.8. We fired 60 shells in little over 2 minutes & only 4 early faults [to shew?] in their attempts alternating further 2 M.G.S.	
19		2/8 Reworks relieved in R/M subsect by 2/5 Rework. Shots fired 170. (1) On N. we fired during afternoon and evening on S.S.30, 6.45 and 8.45 thoroughly searching enemy rear in front line at M30.a.4.03. We retaliated with H.S. M.T.M. and rifle grenade fall on Sects M.29.3 and a 2/11 & 2/14-29.4.	

T2134. Wt. W708-776. 500000. 4/15. Sir J. C. & S.

WAR DIARY or INTELLIGENCE SUMMARY

Army Form C. 2118.

C/182nd Trench Mortar Battery

August 1916

Place	Date	Hour	Summary of Events and Information	Remarks and references to Appendices
LAVENTIE	20		(a) On S. We registered enemy's craters on Duck's Bill. In afternoon we cooperated with M.T.M's against heavy trench communications trenches at 3.5.6.7½.5. and M.35 c 73 2½/4½. Normal retaliation with equal response at T.M's (unclassified but fairly heavy) fully at sects 3.5.6 and M.35.2. 2/8 Resents report that during this time an S. subsection enemy's activities at T.M's has greatly abated and its own Stokes's Lohr battr. on high and 15th section up 3-5 sheets. We fired in all course 1 st day 159 shells at various points in enemy's front line, causing normal retaliation. Cadet Ryan was picked up and taken the cellar (?) at S.5.b.34. 2nd (b) M.g.E. M.36 c 1½.6. Bell was shelled with shrapnel. To-day 2/Lt Grady returned from Hospital after being found to be improving.	
	21		To-night we let up 150 Stella grenades to Moss's hole. 174 Stella fired in cooperation with M.T.M's and Rifle at 5.30 p.m. also independently throughout day. Enemy's fire also was through bombardment at M. and b sector with moderate retaliation. with normal amount T.M's (Priester), aerial trpedos, and 77 mm shells, showing little change (at enemy's) 150 Stella taken up again to Winchester Saddle).	

Army Form C. 2118.

WAR DIARY
or
INTELLIGENCE SUMMARY.

1/2nd Trench Mortar Battery

(Erase heading not required.)

August 1916

Place	Date	Hour	Summary of Events and Information	Remarks and references to Appendices
LAVENTIE	22		Our new arrangement of pulling D.A.C. shells 150 shells direct to Eglon Dump 5 miles a week, works very well. Coopers and M.T.M.S and 18 pdrs carried firing at intense standard all day. 172 shells expended. Enemy fire heavy at M30 a 3 3/4 to M30 a 6.2. Retaliated on Support line at M30 a 5.9. Retaliation being weak L.T.M., M.T.M, H.S. stopped futher enemy action. On M/g we paid particular attention to Latrine about M36 a 3.8 on line. M36 a 4.4. Retaliation nil. In the evening 150 shells sent up to Moss's Hole.	
	23		In preparation for the heavy programme tomorrow we reconnoitred our front line expending 101 shells. Our trenches during front and support lines from M30 a 3 1/2.4 — M30 a 3 1/2.03, & front line at S.5.6 7/2-7, front and support lines at M36 c 3.8 and front line and communication trench at M36 a 3 1/2 13. Retaliation normal & all attempt fruit.	
	24.		Shots fired 253. During the day in left section we fired at front and support line at M30 a 3.03. On night we fired 4 guns to barrage or extreme left sector to co-ordinate w/ 2/1st Brigade. The signal to open fire was to be explosion in Bavaria Brigade about 10 p.m. The wire cut sector of our aircraft very methodically and kept up our artillery and trench guns in every patrol in makeing the preparation. En cavery quite artfuler very methodically and kept up heavy fire in every patrol	

WAR DIARY or INTELLIGENCE SUMMARY

Army Form C. 2118.

August 1916 9/182nd Trench Mortar Battery

Place	Date	Hour	Summary of Events and Information	Remarks and references to Appendices
LAVENTIE	25	1.10 pm	Col. 1.10 am however, one of the torpedoes was exploded and set operations back to preparation. Retaliation with M. Minenwerfers. SIGNPOST LANE was badly shaken called to its retail. The second round misfired. The first open near SIGNPOST LANE was badly shaken called to its retail. The second round delay, is attrib. to the torn red rockets front-front parapet wire etc. by streams of enemy ??eve fire signal, and fires was stopped for some minutes. But for then his trench a (quite number of shells would have been fired. Shots fired 273. On the night and fired a few line steepens the day, with search of enemy's open communication from M.30 a 6.0 to M.30 c 5.9. Retaliation minor. On Ra/m during day fired on front line at M.35.d 9.4. 2 shells fired rapid successively him covered most turn to fly and was followed by to round & a hour long. Plane is enemy's hand; shown front line at M.36.c.1.6, when checkerboards were seen to fly.	
		6.30 pm	Opens a brisk rapid fire for 3 minutes on following points 443 ① Communication trench and rail head at M36 e 1.6. ② Communication trench as marked at M36 c 2.d. ③ Communic- trench at M35 d 9 3/4. The guns were traversed with any slight alter speed half minute very carefully	

Army Form C. 2118.

WAR DIARY
or
INTELLIGENCE SUMMARY.
(Erase heading not required.)

Instructions regarding War Diaries and Intelligence Summaries are contained in F. S. Regs., Part II. and the Staff Manual respectively. Title pages will be prepared in manuscript.

April 1916.   of 102nd Trench Mortar Battery

Place	Date	Hour	Summary of Events and Information	Remarks and references to Appendices
LAVENTIE				
	26		Storey wounded & taken to Parados. Revolvers very weak, sent back 6 aerial torpedoes and 3 eq 77mm shells.	
	27		Lt Bayard returns to 183 Inf Bing. 1/2 T.M.B. returned to 6W Lines at LA GORGUE.	
	28		10 men sent to instruct as trench gunners for 2/6 Revock	
	29		Guns washed and cleaning rather ye battery. Taking 1 recruit. 2/Lt C.C. Coats 2/6 Revock is attached to instruct vice Lt Phillippi	
	30		2/7 Revock returns to his Battalion.	
	31		2/6 detachment returned to their battalion being replaced by 10 men of 2/8 Revock. General orders.	

D. Morris Capt
OC 102 TMB

www.ingramcontent.com/pod-product-compliance
Lightning Source LLC
Chambersburg PA
CBHW081503160426
43193CB00014B/2574